Inside a blessing

Prayers, Poems and Reflections

Clare Locke

Cover design and illustrations by Clare Locke.

Inside a blessing: Prayers, Poems and Reflections © Clare Locke 2024. All rights reserved. No part of this book may be reproduced or transmitted in any form or by any means, eletronic or mechanical, including photocopying, recording, taping or any retrieval system, without permission in writing from the publishers.

First published in Brisbane, Australia by Clocke Design.

ISBN: 978-0-6459494-0-7

For Mum and Dad, who always reply
and for Andy, who first encouraged me

Contents

I
PRAYER

Threads of light —2
Bathe in light—4
The Strength of Mothers—5
For Mothers—6
For the boys who grow—7
God of birthdays—8
God of peace—9
Awakening purpose—10
Open gate—11
God of struggling plants—12
To pause a while—13
God of light—14
God of new mornings—15
Jesus, patient listener—16
The breath of peace—17
Courage for beginning—18
To be good news—19
Companion and friend—20
Table grace—21
Unconditional Love—22
For tending the soil—23
God of imagination—24

II
LOVE

Love who spoke—26
Down to earth—27
Widow of creation—28
Mary wept—30
Spirit—31
Resting on the earth—32
Gentle Healer—33
Striving yet wounded—34
Mother of light—35
Before light—36
Remembering Wisdom—37
Earth maker—38
Ocean Dweller—39
Breathe child—40
Paradox—41
The garden—42
Bless the sun—43
A small blessing—44
Be gentle with yourself—45
Thank you for the bees—46
Omega—47
One with us—48
I never did it alone—49

III
WONDER

Low tide—52
The wind has changed—54
Clouds in December—55
Sun cure—56
Sun kiss—56
Midweek sunset—57
Amity—58
Bird sweep—59
The idea of rest—60
Pink prawn sky—61
Minjerribah Haikus—62
The baby I held—64
Baby blanket—65
Mother is—66
Even if her name is lost—67
Dreamer—68

IV
MEMORY

They live—70
A low blow—72
Oh my sister—73
Even if her name is lost—74
Mercy—75
Soupy—76
Rain—77
5am rain—78
A persistence of life—79
Beautiful ordinary things—80
3pm storm—81
Sodden—82
Slow brain—83
We go west—84
Between rides—85

I

PRAYER

Threads of light

We gather in your light
Feel your glow in our pulsing blood
Our beating hearts
The bodies of us within the unimaginable
Body of you

Our hurts and hopes
Our strange, beautiful lives
All of it, gathered
Every creature
Everlastingly yours

Who are we in your making?
In your endless creating?

We humans
We stumble
We forget, yet
Everything is eternal in you
Everything becomes in you
All made new, more true

Surprise us
Into the colours of your joy
The deep sound of your compassion
We echo you, graced
And even in the darkest place
Thin threads of hope burn bright

Dancing, remembering
Laughing, crying
Hands reaching hands
We share your light

Bathe in light

It says I'm only lost
If I think I know
Where I'm headed
I picture the sun rising
And my blind attraction to it
Walk to the sun, I say
Through those newly minted glinting waves
Let the young day's warmth kiss
My closed eyelids
My open yearning chest
Let me drown in morning sunshine
Let me bathe in light

The Strength of Mothers

God who is nurturer and protector
Bless all mothers, grandmothers and the women
who love and care for us

Hold in your embrace those who have gone before us
Comfort the mothers who suffer
Give courage to those who struggle

As we celebrate Mothers this day
Let our love for mothers be the model
for our compassion for all people
Born of your great love

May our love be strengthen by the mother
Who so loved her son

For Mothers

We bless our mothers and the women who care for us
Who share our joys and successes
Who comfort us through fear and failure.

We pray for the mothers who grieve for the loss
of loved ones, who suffer due to illness, violence or poverty.

May we uphold their dignity and support their needs.

Through times of hardship and struggle
May our mothers know we love and honour them.

We pray for mothers who have died.
May they rest in peace and our memories of them
rest always in our hearts.

May mothers and all women share in the wisdom of God
who is love

Creator, nurturer, protector.

We give thanks for mothers.

For the boys who grow

For the boys who grow to become men and fathers
The gentle hands that first hold new life
Astonished by love without condition
Striving for maturity through moments of vulnerability and doubt
Offering humour and patience in times of adversity
The effort, the courage, the humility
The journey that all fathers make
The wisdom they share, the stability they provide,
the curiosity they nurture
For fathers who grieve the loss of children,
children who suffer the lack of a father
— pain that awakens our compassion
For men who struggle to be fathers,
whose lives and relationships are fractured
For fathers who have died, loving and loved
For the stories they told, the skills they taught,
the time they gave
May our memories of fathers weave past through present
and be offered to the future

We bless all fathers.

God of birthdays

God of birthdays
Of significant passages and double digits
Of waiting and expectation
Unwrap our hearts and the many colours of our love
For the ones who lift us and sing loudly to our souls
May your infinite love be the size of our joy

God of peace

God of peace
As poppies grow on the land where soldiers lie
Let the hope of peace grow in our hearts
As we remember the human cost of war
May we remember to speak of peace
When we struggle with fear and anger
Remind us of your patient love, that we might bring
healing to our homes, our workplaces, our schools
Be our strength and our calm in the face of difficulty and conflict
God who is peace
Grow with us

Awakening purpose

God of cool westerlies and crisp mornings
Awaken our weekend purpose
Where leisure meets our list of chores
Temper our impatience
Inspire our love of home
Be the seed of our small content

Open gate

Loving God
Let our hearts be open
Like the gate of the shepherd

May we work away the rust and the stiffness
of our stubbornness and fear
as we practise the movement
of a welcoming love

Let the comforting presence of those we love
of the joy of special days
of this tentative opening up of our daily lives
Remind us of your love, already waiting

In your name, we pray.

God of struggling plants

God of plants in too-small pots
Starved and neglected
Whisper to hands willing to feel caked soil
under finger nails
Let the promise of proper nourishment
be the hope of vigour and new growth

God of tiny buds and green shoots
Inspire our labour
Energise our bodies

To pause a while

God of stillness and in-between times
Of breath and silence
Steady and slow us who rush blindly
Strengthen and ready us in the quiet
Of our waiting places
When we pause on the way
Long enough to pay attention
May your love which meets us here
Flow within us and beyond us
To be a gift to the world

God of light

God of all light and all knowing
Within the light of every distant star
The waking beam of every dawn
The warm glow of all our sunsets
Every candle's light
All our cities by night
Deep ocean luminescence
A beetle's iridescence
Let the light we bear in our own being
Shine forth
Joining the lights of all we journey with in life
God of eternal light, through the radiance
of the Spirit and your only Son
Be our guide
Light our way

God of new mornings

God of new mornings, hope dawning
Of night falling and our homeward calling

You are always in our hearts
Yet beyond the horizon of our understanding

Breath into us your stillness and attentiveness
Grant that we may listen better to hear,
Observe better to see, to learn and grow

Give us compassionate, forgiving hearts
That we may offer this day and each other all that we have

And in this moment, may we know the extraordinary gift of your infinite love.

Jesus, patient listener

Jesus, patient listener
You recognised the faith of a stranger
A woman outside your community

Teach us to listen with compassion
To recognise the fears and concerns of others
To acknowledge their strengths
and the richness of their experience

Let our listening lead to healing and understanding
As our faith leads to you.

The breath of peace

Jesus, your warm breath restored your friends' courage
When they were too fearful to go outside

May your breath and message of peace enter us now
Slowing our minds and bodies
So we can shape within ourselves a calm place of love, faith and hope

Come, Holy Spirit

Courage for beginning

Jesus, your friends missed you,
They were uncertain and maybe even afraid after you left.
Yet they knew your work was important and they had a job to do:
To share the message of God's love and forgiveness.

As we face our tasks this week
   returning to school, to work
   stepping out into the world again
Give us courage and comfort,
Knowing you are present in the faces of friends and strangers.

May we too be your light to the world at this time of change.

To be good news

Jesus, you sent your followers out to the world
As your Father sent you
To be good news

When good news is harder to find
You are still good news

May we who know you, with the gifts we are given
Be good news.

Companion and friend

Jesus, our companion and friend
You left to return to God
Yet you stayed as a light to guide us
Showing us a way to live and love
Let each day bring us closer to you through our care for others
And our care for our common home

Table grace

Jesus of good food and table fellowship
Companion in the meal we share
You broke bread with your friends
So they might remember
To keep the practice
Of gathering
Saying thanks and eating
Bread into body
Energy for life
A communion of hands dusted with flour from the grain
of the green growth of the quiet earth

For this mysterious grace
We give thanks

Unconditional Love

Jesus our brother
You loved your family and friends
You loved strangers who needed you
You even loved people who betrayed you
At this time of fear and worry
May we try to love more like you
As we listen to stories of your life, may we be reminded
of God the Father's great love for you
And God's love for us all
No matter what

For tending the soil

Jesus, you understood and respected
the land of your ancestors,
the ways of farming well, and how life
must be nourished to thrive.

As we are guided by your example
Help us prepare our hearts to be good soil
With patience and vigilance
let us plant and tend the seeds
that grow to produce the fruit that strengthen us all

God of imagination

God of imagination
When we are too weary for study or the effort of work
Whisper to our hearts
Of all you know
The reach of the furthest stars
The impossible power of the tiniest creature
Fill us with wonder
That we might be students of your creation

II

LOVE

Love who spoke

Love who spoke
Into history the story
Already billions of years told
Heard in seeds and soil
On lakes and mountains
In those kneeling to wash another's dirty feet
Bending to tend messy wounds
Running to embrace the bodies
Of once rejected children

Your son's love in you became the story of the Spirit
Awoken in hearts
Spoken in community
Woven in memory and tradition

Great storyteller
May our lives tell the story
Of your eternal love

Down to earth

The earth turns
And I fall off
Deep into night
It's so black and cold
I close my eyes
Now the air is liquid as ocean
And salty too
I am swimming in my tears
Until a voice breaks the void
Breathing me in
To a nested place
The mouth of a tunnel
With a soft entrance and soft walls
Like the endless belly of a worm
Yet I flow and move
A slender vessel
Down to land
On leaves. Soft brown rotted
Smell of earth
I fell and I found her
Oh my beautiful earth
I have loved you
Not well

Widow of creation

Widow of creation
Hold the bodies
Of our vanishing birds
Frogs and small mammals

Weep for the lost plants
The bleached coral
The dying ravaged places

By your tears
Remember

With your sorrow
Enfold them

Wail for all things
Which can never again
Be born in you

Turn to us
Wild mother
We who look away
Tell us the story
Of this suffering earth
Of your wounded heart

Love us still
Your children
Teach us to
Mourn with you

Mary wept

Mary wept
Her boy
He'd left her for the temple long ago
Wandered into the lives
Of the broken and forgotten
They followed him
But he was still her boy
   Her wondering hesitant yes
   Her unexpected change
   Her unending joy and worry
   Her dying boy
For a moment there
While she held him
The broken weight of him
The blood and dust of him
She remembers the beginning
The gasping cries
The living breath
Of her baby boy

Spirit

Energy of love
Goodness like fire
Burn bright our hearts

Breath of life
Seek us, wake us,
Move us with your
Impatient air

River from the source
Surge and flow
Nourish the dry
Where green unfurls

Bird of joy
Wing your way
Sing your day
Make the world

Resting on the earth

As if we were babies
Once more
We lean back against hands
Which have only ever loved us
Into the milky white
The last light
Of soft acceptance
Blind and without need
We rest on the grass
Covering the dark earth
Until our flesh feeds the roots
Of the blossoming tree
Our bones keep her company
And every wriggling worm and tiny bacterium
Silently praises the one
Who made death so becoming
To life

Gentle Healer

Gentle Healer
You hold us in your love
Listen, we pray,
To our hurts and heartache
To our frustrations and fears
Be our comfort when living feels hard
And when days stretch long
Sooth our tired bodies
Our foggy brains
So that when night falls
And our work is done
We may sleep, deep in
The peace of you.

Striving yet wounded

Intimate cellular love
All in all
You delight to
Activate the organism
Warm the rock
Fill and flow
Thrive in the heaving breathing
Lungs
And we echo your agency
Emulate
Strive to know yet
Warring and wounded
Shadow the sun
Hang life from the beam
Of her fallen tree

Mother of light

Light is nearly born
Night is breathing deeper
Light cries out at
The effort of its radiance
Making morning
Bird song
Bringing all things into
Being
All things seen and perceived
Are received
The people lean towards the day
And it washes them
Poured from the apse of the sky
The mother of light
Weeps at the sight
She sees what they see
The dawn of life
Love into eternity

Before light

Before light there was hope
An idea of the shape of things
Emerging slowly in greys into colour
Before breath there was a shimmer
Ready for rising, moving, flowing
Wind blowing
Before birdsong a waiting silence
Immensity of words unspoken
Sleep unbroken
Before waking, in dreaming
Life began

Remembering Wisdom

She ran childlike in the grass
Laughing
Shedding her joy in particles of light
Barefoot in mud, relishing the mess
She was first, always
Love's companion
Feeling her way into every created thing
Under the skin of it all
Spinning with planets and atoms
Falling with rain
Flowing with rivers
Soaking the soil
Vivid, alive
Delighting the sprouting seeds, beetles and worms
Who sing her song
Mimic her dance
Spontaneous and graceful
Her echo in creation
Now a yearning, a glimmering
A bright remembering
Of wisdom

Earth maker

Earth maker
Push and shape
Speak what you create
Water mixed in the dust
From the crust
The cooled skin
Above the hot muscle of rock
Ocean covered
You formed this
An eye for perfection and
Two hands to
Stroke the warm belly
Of life conceived
Kin for kin
Your breath begins
And we are
This teeming earth

-after Irenaeus

Ocean Dweller

Ocean Dweller
You are within and beyond
The vast depths
And is that you, sleeping unafraid in the boat we struggle in?
We cry out, floundering
Amidst hammering waves
And blackened skies
If we fall, do we drown with you?
How cold it is
How afraid we are
How do we live like this?
To trust without truly knowing
To sail on, with you
Our heart's companion
Towards the horizon of wordlessness

Breathe child

Breathe child
Let it be a seed
Small works, small deeds
Not all will flow
But move slow
Love is in noticing

Paradox

Who knew emptiness
Could be so full
Space expanding limitlessly
Gift offered endlessly
To all which grows and dies
Made new and new again
The unknowable becoming known, obscurely
Always pouring self
Towards inventiveness
Creation's mouth wide open hungry
Divinity swallowed whole
Absorbed in life's infinite expressions
Into the bloodstream and the bleeding
Of Earth and its creatures
Changed and changing
Belonging with it all
Beyond it all
And all things reaching for home

The garden

Flowers grow
In each heart a garden
A patchwork of light and life
Of our joys and cares
Hopes and sorrows
These bud and bloom
As one wilts another grows
With compassion and patience
We tend and rest
Tend and rest
And then, with gentle invitation
Kindness and curiosity
We weed the paths
That connect us
And walk amidst the wonder
Of so many blazing colours

Bless the sun

Bless the sun
Shining on the crepe myrtle leaves
The dancing gumtree which welcomes the parrots
Stretching her limbs up to the blue

I saw bees in the nasturtiums this morning
Thank God, still there!
They sooth despair

The shrubs nearby are breathing out the breeze, a long soft
Fffffffffff

A crow calls a solitary note
Amidst the small bird twitters and road noise

Work waits
But I won't leave yet
My meditation keeps me here
Inside a blessing

A small blessing

A small blessing snuck up the rain
She's shedding herself like snow
Tiny tufts of cotton cloud
Bright white on the soaked dark earth
Green shoots dance worship around her trunk
This morning in the glisten
After days of rain
This is her moment

Be gentle with yourself

Be gentle with yourself
Brush the cruel voice from your shoulder
She's after the soft spots
the pain points

Be gentle with yourself
The world is mad this way
We're all dropping stitches
And untangling knots

Be gentle and walk
The sun is somewhere in the blue
And birds who never plan lunch
Are flying overhead

Be gentle and be amazed
At the breath filling your chest
The cool inhale
The warm exhale that softens your face

Be gentle and notice
Your hand has a hand for a friend

Thank you for the bees

Thank you for the bees

The trees

Skinned knees

Birds

And words

That build us

Connect us

Leave us with kindness

And the desire to be here

Tomorrow

Omega

O my eager soul
Leans into your endless beckoning
Your whispering
Always towards the next day
The new way
Of becoming

One with us

We borrow this time
Our joy and sorrow spoken
Into the ear of your earth
This moment, in this bodily form
Fleeting within your eternity
Who are you?
I am with all things
I am compassion
Tenderly, life unfolds in me
I enfold life
Offering the milk of love
I kiss your wounds

We walk briefly here
Breath the glow of your air
Our hopes join past to new
Fragile yet enduring
In silence and song
All is praise
For grace

I never did it alone

It is a song
A yearning
A delighted sense of undeserving
A gap in knowledge
Yet all I know
As breathing is certain
And life both fast and slow
Every cycle
Of lungs and thought expelled
The world and its air consumed
Is the taking and disposal of a gift:
I never did it alone

III

WONDER

Low tide

He calls them convoys
The armies of soldier crabs
Scuttling and scattering on whispering legs
Or hurriedly burying their bodies
In the watery sand at our feet

Fish flit and brown sea cucumbers lie
Unappetisingly still in remnant tidal puddles
Amidst slimy sea grass
Hiding treacherous holes

We meander up the dark mouth of
The mangrove lined river
It's a tea tree infused bath
"Filled with God's wee" we laugh
As we wade along, shimmering the silken surface
Too noisy with our natter to hear
The quiet chatter of unseen birds
But glimpses of the scene are enough
The bend of dark mangrove roots
Sprouting glossy green leaves
Their shifting shade brightening the water's golden light
And the soft mattress of sand below our toes

We turn back towards the flats
To the sun's rays slanting
Across the ripples of muddy sand
The ebbing, retreating ocean
And the endless convoys of crabs

The wind has changed

The wind has changed overnight

Bringing cool air and stirring the water

Tiny fish swerve in schools

Around the jetty

Where at our feet the tuna's fin flickers, blood leaking from its gills

The fisherman scoops buckets of water to wash clean the bloodied scene

His success in battle with the muscly fish has excited others to hope they too might land a prize

Rods and lines are flicking into the wind

The pelican gazes on with cormorants nearby and osprey overhead

Dolphins glide near the surface, and down again

While the wind chops the water

And we hold our hats

Only the sky is unmoved

A dome of unending blue

Clouds in December

A grey milkiness
Masks the sun's summer intention
A black cat slinks into a storm drain where
Weeds sprout and frangipani flowers fall

I pass by swaying green leaves
And insect noise rising like a
Near boiling pot of water

A fluttering butterfly could be a bird
While real birds are stationary
Perched on overhead wires
Lulled by the holiday limbo
Listless in the year's last days

Pin pricks on my face
Of wet blown to cool
The ruffling gusts meet the warm stillness
Of a morning subdued
Yet so thoroughly alive

Sun cure

The sun will cure me
The wind soft and the coo of the dove
Gentle pendulum of the sheets on the line
Blurred roar from the road above
Sit here and want nothing
Nothing wanted of me
But simple attention

Sun kiss

Spent a fleeting moment
Standing in the sun
Kissed me on the neck

Midweek sunset

Alongside the Thai takeaway is a patch of forest
An odd mix of figs with snaking buttress roots
And tall white-limbed eucalypts
Breaking through to sky

Here the noise of a train mingles with cars, trucks
and the air conditioner purr of the suburbs
From the pocket of dim-lit trees comes the hum and hush
of crickets and breeze

It's anticipatory, yet slow
A midweek evening of people travelling home
Engines idling at drive-thru windows
Sky with brushstroke clouds, dipping sun and birds flying over
Calling day's last chorus

Such soft majesty as day closes
The sunset answer to a sunrise question
And so it was

Amity

The turquoise water glints and sparkles
Impossible as a tourism ad
The old and overweight bring their noodles
Bobbing serenely
Water hats clipped under chins
Kids dig holes in sand the tide will fill and smooth
Brown skinned boys in boardies backflip off the jetty
A red bikini woman perches on a boat pulled up the ramp by a 4WD
Jet skiers, snorkelers
Wet haired girls in fluoro rashies
All is splash and chatter
In the hot high sun
And the sky
Day lit blue
Endless above

Bird sweep

Birds stretch the sky small silhouettes in clans and hustling clusters
Black wire lines loop the sweep paused by the fluff tuft of a self cleaning bird
Twitching with little nitty itch
Small black against
This pale blue
Before the sun brings full colour
And it's filling now
Painting the greens, the blond dog
The upright goodmorning trees

The idea of rest

I've found the perfect pocket of time
Where I can pretend with sleepy eyed calm
That afternoons like this never end.
Movement is small and soft as breathing
Birds call outside and the plaster walls gently creak
I'm resistant to the thought of being anywhere else
Than here, where sunlight and shadow alternate through the blinds
I could sleep. I would.
But time moves after all.
The rest was pleasurable for being so fleeting
As if the idea was enough

Pink prawn sky

Pink prawn sky
Embryonic clouds
Growing, mutating
The last splendid sun soaked cloud
Drama at the heart
Mauve and blue in the chorus
—Was there ever such a sunset?
A cloud pyre on fire
Til embers dim
And it is gone

Minjerribah Haikus

Waves curl dolphins play
Along the edge of the beach
Our eyes are searching

Blue butterflies chase
Spiralling amongst green leaves
My heart follows them

Sun rests in my skin
Wind and trees talk in whispers
This is all I need

Walk the unknown road
To where sky opens to sand
Felled trees like antlers

Grevillea hums
The pink brushes blessed with bees
And butterflies too

What joy to watch bees
Climbing the pink brush flowers
Yellow on their knees

A holiday ends
I hold the taste of salt air
Take sunlight back home

The baby I held

The baby I held in the chair
His hair
Meets my cheek
I kiss his head
Breathe the twelve year old smell of him
His long arms wrap me
And in the seconds of stillness
I remember the baby I held
As the sun rose

Baby blanket

I smooth the small blanket over
my son's sleep ready body
A woollen grid of coloured granny squares
Crocheted years ago when the pregnancy
Hung on by a thread
The doctor demanded rest
And rest needed a focus
To learn a skill well enough
To create one faulty square after another
As days past and the baby grew
From impossible to premature
Life continuing in a plastic box
Attached to beeping machines
Via a tangle of cords
Nested, chest rising and falling
As he is nested now
With his face buried
Between pillow and blankets
And I'm drawn to his comfort,
His soft sleepy safety
To whisper goodnight and breath his shampooed hair and warm body
I stroke the blanket
Remembering how it grew and draped over my belly in those waiting weeks
Emerging as a promise to my son

Mother is

The mother is a mine
In the rock and soil
Extract the baby
The baby extracts her milk

The mother is the ocean
Full of tears not wept
She's reflecting your blue sky
Your grey clouds

The mother is tree
In a forest of trees who whisper
Why does it hurt to love?
Before the axe falls

The mother is flesh
Ageing into lines
Of loss and laughter
She belongs to time

Even if her name is lost

Life needs soil
And we are it
The women who bear
Those born
To thirst and hunger
The cord is cut
But never broken
I knew your mother
And your mother's mother
Even if her name is lost
And her body dust
She carried your men
She grieved at their tomb
She held your children
In the room
Of her swollen heart
Remember this:
You were her child

Dreamer

The man stands on his block
A rectangular portion of hill
His white SUV parked on the road below
alongside temporary fencing
One arm lifted to support a sun shielding hand
Summer morning bright and the jarring jangle of my passing train
Stills him
He imagines the house he'll build on the purchase
Where grass and weeds grow
And we know- steadily, sturdily
His home will rise
For now, only the sun aches to touch
his dreaming face

IV

MEMORY

They live

So well did they live
That the land seemed
To unseeing latecomers
Empty of their impact
They had walked and loved
Tenderly, reverently
Watching well
Knowing when the slightest change came
What it would share
Using hands and learned ways
Of bringing forth
All good things
Life flowing from mother to daughter
Father to son
When wisdom spoke the people attended
Held the stories of their ancestors
They danced, sang and painted
And nothing was broken
That could not be healed

The shadow of the boats
Spread disease, sprayed bullets
And new words
Weasel words
Unfaithful deeds
Death was an end for many but could not explain
The horror
The inhumanity
The land who laments her children
Those she knew who knew her seasons
The intimacy of long love
The strangers stole
And wrote the laws
To limit and eliminate
As if those who were first might be gone
Forgotten fossils
But they are not
They live
Strong in land and lore which has held their hopes
Their memories
Their ways
And the strangers speak of the shame of their past
The undoing which must be undone
The hands outstretched, unarmed
And ears listening
To voices
Who speak
This is us

A low blow

A low blow
We said no
The echo
Of a face slap
A thunderclap
A bone snap
A push back
A whip crack
A head whack
Then silence

Oh my sister

Oh my sister
Your life in the hands of a mister
Outside shrouded
Outside muted
Outside deleted
The four walls of your home are
Your whole damn life
Your body to cook and clean and bring his babies into the world
Oh my sister
You went to school once
You caught the bus once
You had a future once
What hell to be a daughter
What sorrow to be a sister

Even if her name is lost

Life needs soil
And we are it
The women who bear
Those born
To thirst and hunger
The cord is cut
But never broken
I knew your mother
And your mother's mother
Even if her name is lost
And her body dust
She carried your men
She grieved at their tomb
She held your children
In the room
Of her swollen heart
Remember this:
You were her child

Mercy

The sun's bleaching the clothes summer baked crispy edged hot
to touch better get the washing off the line it's so bloody hot
my brain's leaking fluid as an offering to the fierce golden ball and
my boiling blood is crying mercy mercy mercy

Soupy

Soupy days and nights
Storms crackle impressively in the distance
A light show passing to the west
Leaving our air thick and damp and exhausting
We complain and secretly love
Our way of being summered
Hugged too long by a sweaty friend
Who we know will let go in the end
The muggy stillness releases us
From the effort of caring too much
Or moving or thinking
We even blink more slowly
The tap water seems thick, mucousy to swallow
Only the fridge
The beautiful fridge
Whispers cool promises
Of grapes and orange juice with ice cubes
Fleeting, dissolving
Til we return to be lulled by insects and the lush
Warm weight of January

Rain

It rains
The small hits of every drip
Crescendo and weightier now
Licks and flicks off leaves
Some crystal drops hang glimmer globes bright and heavy
And down
They fall
This tall curtain of rain
Scrubbing at my near sky
Dancing on the grass floor

Decrescendo and the glow
Of the sun on the shoulder
Of the grey day
Til the lighter littlest drips
Fade away

5am rain

Midnight rain. 5am rain.
Tattoo on my brain
The drum beat
The wet ink
Repetitive. Indelible.
   A chorus like a ward of sleepless babies
And I want to cry too
   Let me sleep!
But it's the rain
She's deaf and deafening
Unrestrained
At midnight. 5am.

A persistence of life

We return home to a garden overgrown
After days of rain and heat
The vegetation has inched toward overthrow
And we fight back
With lawn mowers
Whipper snippers
Pull at weeds and the runners of over-enthusiastic grass
on a mission to seek new ground
My neighbour muses that
If humans were gone
If we were out of the equation
The plants and animals would creep back into our concrete world
I picture weeds and tree roots cracking open the roads
A persistence of life
A beautiful conquest

Beautiful ordinary things

The rain will come
But today is bright
With birds and wallabies
Roadside plums and green glowing foliage of unidentified shrubs
We walk talking of birds
Keeping our plums in our pockets
Joggers pass
A twitchy horse with its snowy haired rider
Men on mountain bikes
My sons and I follow the path
Noticing ruby tree sap
Brown butterflies
Blow flies
A friendly kelpie
Weeds and gravel
Rabbits
A walk becomes a list of such beautiful ordinary things
It is Christmas tomorrow
All things come into world
Look

3pm storm

Emerge from the undercover carpark
Into torrential rain
Sweeping sheets obscuring vision
And roads now dangerous fast flowing rivers
Gritting teeth, gripping the wheel
Pass the sensible drivers pulled over to wait out the wildness
But this woman is homeward bound, half a suburb to go
Focused but frankly afraid of
The surging, swelling water
The drum beat in the sky and
The flashing fury of a 3pm storm

Sodden

Rain falls on the roadside couches
Soaks through the faded fabric cushions
Finds the gaps in the cracks of the tired black leather
They're waiting for a truck
Like passengers for a bus
Solid props for leaning bookcases and swollen MDF shelves
Old entertainment units
Electric fans and plastic trikes
Sagging mattresses and
So many other unwanted belongings
All sinking into the earth
Sodden and sorrowful
While all around the grass grows
And the gutters run

Slow brain

Do you have a slow brain
Like me?
Getting lost in low lit corridors of thought
Searching for an old classroom or an old friend
But it's all changed
Renovated
And the friend left years ago
And I wander
I wonder
How did I ever survive being so slow?
Watching waves muddle the sand
Listening to an early bird one day
And the next and the next
I'll play with the sand
Each fine grain worth the trouble
Run my hands through seeded grass
Drink the golden orange juice of the sun in all the daylit places

It's the fast lane I'm worried about
Crushed by the rush of quick thinkers
Snappy deciders
How did I ever survive?

We go west

Saturday train
The sliding amber sun gleaming
Brightly the signs and tree tops
We go west
Funnelling
Swallowing up the day
Drinking up the light
Pouring towards the hills
To home

Between rides

The Uber driver has parked his car
In a quiet street
Of a quiet suburb
He's quietly standing on the grass between
The road and the overgrown creek
Where he has placed his patterned prayer mat
The sun is deep in the west
The moon is a delicate slice
And he's facing that way
Kneeling that way
Arms outstretched, head low
Palms towards the earth

www.ingramcontent.com/pod-product-compliance
Lightning Source LLC
Chambersburg PA
CBHW062053290426
44109CB00027B/2812